ENDANGERED
RHINOCEROS

Bobbie Kalman
Crabtree Publishing Company
www.crabtreebooks.com

Earth's Endangered Animals Series

A Bobbie Kalman Book

Dedicated by Andrea Crabtree
Debby McDowall—It is a privilege being friends with you.
You are brave and confident, and you set such a wonderful example—Love Andrea

Author and Editor-in-Chief
Bobbie Kalman

Research
Kristina Lundblad

Substantive editor
Kathryn Smithyman

Editors
Kelley MacAulay
Rebecca Sjonger

Design
Bobbie Kalman
Samantha Crabtree (cover and title page)
Katherine Kantor

Production coordinator
Heather Fitzpatrick

Photo research
Crystal Foxton

Consultant
Patricia Loesche, Ph.D., Animal Behavior Program,
Department of Psychology, University of Washington

Special thanks to
World Wildlife Fund (WWF)

Photographs
Cincinnati Zoo and Botanical Garden: David Jenike:
    pages 22-23, 28, 29
Bruce Coleman Inc.: Dieter & Mary Plage: page 25
Visuals Unlimited: Joe McDonald: page 21
Bharat Pokharel/WWF-Nepal: page 27 (top)
Lee Poston/WWF: page 27 (bottom)
Other images by Corel, Digital Stock, and Digital Vision

Illustrations
Barbara Bedell: back cover, border, pages 4, 5, 6, 7, 8,
    9 (except horse and zebra), 10, 17, 18, 21, 24, 30
Jeannette McNaughton-Julich: page 9 (horse and zebra)

Digital prepress
Embassy Graphics

Printer
Worzalla Publishing

Crabtree Publishing Company

www.crabtreebooks.com   1-800-387-7650

PMB 16A	612 Welland Avenue	73 Lime Walk
350 Fifth Avenue	St. Catharines	Headington
Suite 3308	Ontario	Oxford
New York, NY	Canada	OX3 7AD
10118	L2M 5V6	United Kingdom

Cataloging-in-Publication Data
Kalman, Bobbie.
  Endangered rhinoceros / Bobbie Kalman.
    p. cm. -- (Earth's endangered animals series)
  Includes index.
  ISBN 0-7787-1852-2 (RLB) -- ISBN 0-7787-1898-0 (pbk.)
 1. Rhinoceroses--Juvenile literature. 2. Endangered species--
Juvenile literature. [1. Rhinoceroses. 2. Endangered species.]
I. Title.
  QL737.U63K25 2004
  599.66'8--dc22
                                   2003025589
                                     LC

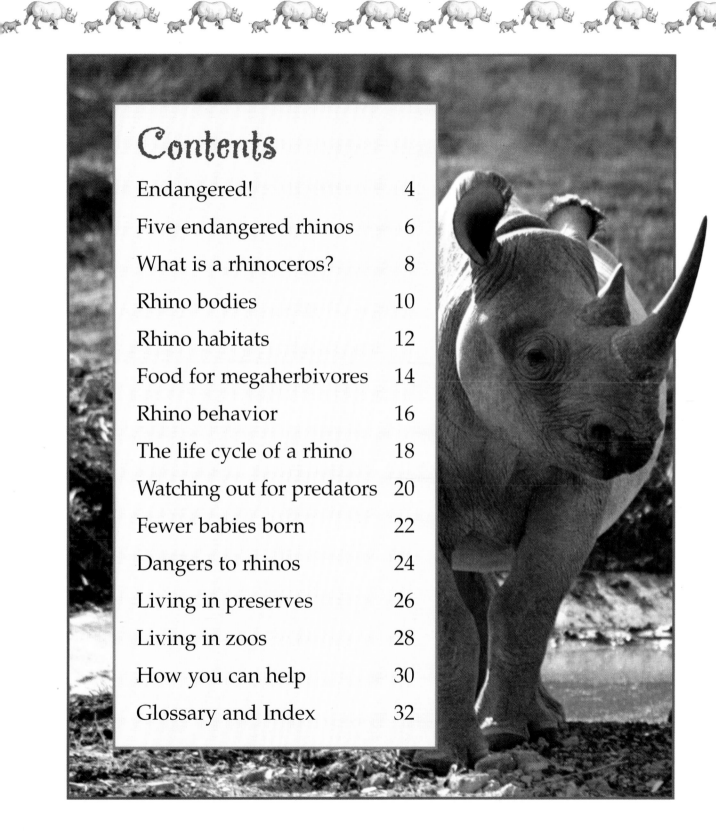

Contents

Endangered!

There are more than 1,000 known **species**, or types, of **endangered** animals on Earth today. In a few more years, many of these species will become **extinct**. All rhinoceros are endangered, and some species are in danger of becoming extinct in the near future. Find out more about the different species of rhinoceros, why these animals are endangered, and how people can help them.

The black rhinoceros, or rhino, is one of the most endangered rhinos.

Words to know

Scientists use special words to describe animals in danger. Read and find out what the words below mean.

extinct Describes animals that have died out and have not been seen for at least 50 years in the **wild**, or places that are not controlled by people

extinct in the wild Describes animals that survive only in zoos or other areas managed by people

critically endangered Describes animals that are at high risk of dying out in the wild

endangered Describes animals that are in danger of dying out in the natural places where they live

vulnerable Describes animals that may become endangered because they face certain dangers where they live

5

Five endangered rhinos

There are five species of rhinos. Some are critically endangered. In fact, the Javan rhinoceros may be gone from the wild in fewer than ten years. Not only is it the most endangered rhino, it may be the most endangered **mammal** in the world!

Sumatran rhinoceros

Javan rhinoceros

Javan rhinoceros are critically endangered. Fewer than 60 of these rhinos are alive today. They live in two places in the world. One group is in Java, Indonesia, and the other is in Vietnam. The Javan rhino is also known as the "Asian lesser one-horned rhinoceros."

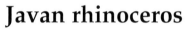

Javan rhinoceros

Sumatran rhinoceros

The Sumatran rhinoceros is critically endangered. There are fewer than 300 of these rhinos alive today in the countries of Indonesia and Malaysia. This animal is also known as the "hairy rhino" and the "Asian two-horned rhinoceros" because it has patches of long shaggy hair and two horns. Sumatran rhino babies are covered in thick black hair. (See pictures of Sumatran rhino babies on pages 28 and 29.)

Black rhinoceros

The black rhinoceros has two horns and a hooked, pointed upper lip. It is also known as the "hooked-lip rhinoceros." Its thick, gray, hairless **hide**, or skin, is usually covered with mud or dust, making this rhino appear black. The black rhinoceros lives in Africa. There are fewer than 2,500 of these animals still alive. Scientists believe that, without help, this rhino may be extinct by the year 2010.

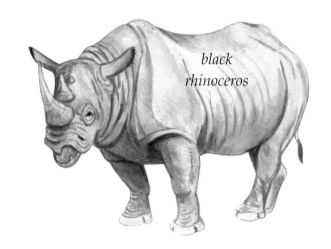

black rhinoceros

White rhinoceros

The white rhinoceros also has two horns and lives in Africa. Between 11,000 and 12,000 of these rhinos live in two separate groups. One group, called the northern group, is critically endangered. The other group, called the southern group, has increased in numbers.

Indian rhinoceros

The Indian, or "Asian greater one-horned rhino," is larger than the Javan, or "Asian lesser one-horned rhino." The Indian rhino has one horn and big, knobby armor-like plates covering its body. It also has large folds of skin at its neck. Thanks to people in India and Nepal, who worked hard to save this rhino, the number of Indian rhinoceros has grown from 200 to 2,400!

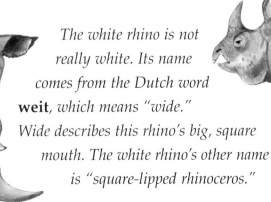

white rhinoceros

The white rhino is not really white. Its name comes from the Dutch word **weit***, which means "wide." Wide describes this rhino's big, square mouth. The white rhino's other name is "square-lipped rhinoceros."*

Indian rhinoceros

What is a rhinoceros?

A rhinoceros is a mammal. Mammals are **warm-blooded** animals. The bodies of warm-blooded animals stay about the same temperature, no matter how warm or cold their surroundings are. Mammals have backbones, and some have hair or fur on their bodies. Female mammals feed their babies milk from their bodies.

*Rhinos love to **wallow** in mud. Wallowing, or rolling around in mud and water, helps keep rhinos cool. The mud coating on their skin also protects rhinos from flies that try to bite them.*

Odd-toed and even-toed hoofs

Rhinoceros belong to a group of animals called **ungulates**. Ungulates are mammals with hooves. There are two groups of ungulates—**artiodactyls** and **perissodactyls**. Artiodactyls are even-toed ungulates. They have hooves with two toes. Giraffes, hippopotamuses, and deer are artiodactyls. Perissodactyls are odd-toed ungulates.

one toe

three toes

Their hooves have either one or three toes. Horses, zebras, tapirs, and rhinos are perissodactyls. Horses and zebras have one toe, whereas rhinos and tapirs have three toes.

horse

tapir

zebra

rhinoceros

9

Rhino bodies

Rhinoceros means "horn-nosed," but rhino horns are not really noses, nor are they true horns. Horns are made of bone, but a rhino "horn" is made of **keratin** fibers, which are attached to the skin of the rhino's snout.

Rhino horns can be from one inch (2.5 cm) to over five feet (1.5 m) long! They are used mainly in fighting, but rhinos may also use them to dig up plant roots for food.

Rhinos have one or two horns.

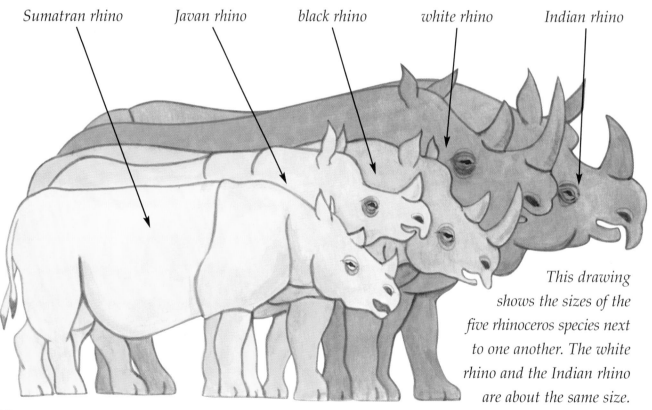

Sumatran rhino   Javan rhino   black rhino   white rhino   Indian rhino

This drawing shows the sizes of the five rhinoceros species next to one another. The white rhino and the Indian rhino are about the same size.

Front teeth

Sumatran, Javan, and Indian rhinos have **incisors**, or front cutting teeth, but white and black rhinoceros do not. They use their lips to tear off food.

white rhino

Rhino senses

A rhinoceros does not have good eyesight. Since its eyes are on opposite sides of its head, it can use only one eye at a time to see straight ahead. A rhino has keen senses of smell and hearing, however. These other senses help make up for the rhino's poor eyesight.

Hooked lips

The black rhinoceros, shown above, has a **prehensile** upper lip. A prehensile lip is pointed and hooks under slightly, helping the rhino grab food more easily from trees and shrubs. The Indian rhinoceros, shown below, has a shorter prehensile upper lip than that of the black rhino. When it is eating grasses, it folds back the tip of its lip.

Rhinos have thick folds of skin on their bodies. The Indian rhino's skin looks just like a heavy coat of armor, as shown right.

11

Rhino habitats

A **habitat** is the natural place in which a plant or an animal lives. Rhino habitats include forests, mountains, and **savannas**. Savannas are grassland areas that are scattered with trees.

Rhino habitats always include water. Rhinos go to a watering hole every day to drink, but water sources can dry up. When this happens, rhinos can survive up to four days without water.

These white rhinos live on a savanna in Africa. Savannas are warm during most of the year.

Asian rhino habitats

Javan, Sumatran, and Indian rhinoceros live in Asia. The Javan rhino likes dense rain forests that have water and mud nearby. The Sumatran rhino lives in forested areas, either on hills or in **lowlands**. The Indian rhino, shown right, lives in marshy areas with tall reeds and grasses.

African rhino habitats

Both black rhinos and white rhinos live on savannas in eastern and southern Africa. Black rhinos, shown right, live where there are trees and shrubs to eat, whereas white rhinos, shown opposite, stick to grassy areas. Most Asian rhinos live near water, whereas African rhinos may have to walk several hours to find a watering hole.

13

Food for megaherbivores

Rhinoceros are **herbivores**. Herbivores are animals that eat plants. **Grazers** are herbivores that eat grasses. Only the white rhino is a true grazer. The other rhinos are mainly **browsers**. Browsers eat the branches and leaves of bushes and trees.

Rhinos are **megaherbivores**, or very large herbivores. They eat a huge amount of food every day! Megaherbivores are very important to Earth. They help keep grasses and other plants in their habitats healthy. They also help many kinds of plants grow.

Rhinos look for food in the morning and in the evening, when it is cooler to walk around. They sleep during the hottest times of the day. Black rhinos usually have birds called oxpeckers or tickbirds perched on their bodies. The birds eat the fleas and ticks that live on the skins of rhinos.

Slightly different diets

Besides eating leaves and branches, Javan and Sumatran rhinos also eat bamboo shoots and fruits such as figs and mangos that have fallen from trees. The Indian rhino eats leaves and water plants, but it also grazes on long grasses. Sometimes it raids the crops of farms located near its habitat.

Competing for food

Rhino habitats were once large places with plenty of grass and other plants. Today, however, people are building farms and cities where rhinos live. As people move into rhino habitats, less food is available to rhinos. Rhinos must now compete with one another—and humans—for food. (See page 25.)

Rhino behavior

Most rhinoceros are **solitary**, or prefer to live alone, but mother rhinos keep their babies near them. White rhinos are more social than the other species and often live in **herds**, or groups. Young rhinoceros, such as the black rhinos above, sometimes form small groups.

There may be more than one rhino in a **territory**, but there is only one **dominant** male, or a male that is in charge. The dominant male is usually the one with the largest horn. It marks its territory by spraying urine or dropping its waste along the boundaries.

Charge!

Rhinoceros are peaceful, unless they are threatened. Male rhinos will, however, fight one another over territory or food. Their horns or teeth can cause large wounds. The black rhino is known to **charge**, especially at humans. The Indian rhino also charges. The white rhino may be large, but it is easily frightened. It usually avoids fights.

The black rhino can be aggressive!

*Sometimes a **submissive** white rhino male challenges the dominant male to become dominant. The two rhinos touch horns and stare silently. Then they separate and wipe their horns on the ground. They repeat this behavior until one rhino backs down. Fights rarely happen. The male that wins the challenge becomes dominant and marks the territory. Submissive males do not mark territories.*

The life cycle of a rhino

Every animal goes through a **life cycle**. A life cycle is made up of all the changes that happen to an animal from the time it is born to the time it becomes an adult that can make babies of its own. With each baby, a new life cycle begins.

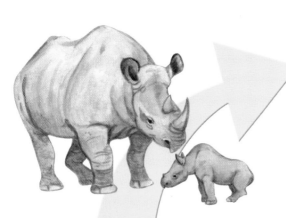

*When a new **calf**, or baby, is born, it **nurses**, or drinks its mother's milk.*

The calf grows. It eats leaves, grasses, or other plant foods. It stays with its mother for about two years.

A female rhino carries her calf inside her body until the baby is ready to be born.

*The **juvenile** rhino then leaves its mother to find a new territory. When it is an adult, it finds a **mate**, or a partner with which it will make babies.*

Ready to mate

In the wild, male rhinos are ready to **mate**, or make babies, between the ages of six and twelve years, but first they have to claim a territory.

Female rhinos

Most female rhinos start mating between four and seven years of age. Female Indian rhinos can have babies when they are three years old, however.

One calf at a time

A rhinoceros calf grows inside its mother's body for fifteen to sixteen months. Rhino mothers usually give birth to one calf every two to four years.

The newborn rhino

At birth, a calf weighs 75 to 150 pounds (34-68 kg) and is about two feet (60 cm) tall. It is helpless and needs its mother for food and protection.

Watching out for predators

Growing rhino calves are watched constantly by their mothers. A female rhino will fight if her calf is threatened by a **predator**. Predators are animals that kill other animals for food.

The predators of black and white rhinos are lions, hyenas, and cheetahs. Asian rhinos have no natural predators. By far the greatest predators of all rhinos, however, are humans.

If a rhino mother is killed, its calf may die as well without food or protection.

Where are the calves?

To protect her baby, a white rhino mother, shown above, keeps the calf in front of her. On the open savanna, predators chase from behind. If a predator was hunting the calf, it would have to deal with the mother before it could attack the baby. A black rhino mother, shown right, stays in front of her calf.

Black rhinos, which look for food among trees and bushes, might find a predator hiding there. With her calf behind her, a black rhino mother could fight the predator and keep the baby safe.

Fewer babies born

Population is the total number of animals in a species. The population of all rhino species is dropping quickly. One of the reasons for the drop is that there are not enough rhinoceros babies that will grow into adults.

Fewer rhinos

When rhino babies die, it takes a long time for their mothers to have new babies. Each year, more rhinos die than are born. When not enough babies are born, fewer rhinos are left on Earth. Without help, some rhino species will become extinct in fewer than twenty years.

Not all the rhino calves that are born grow up to be adults because many are killed.

The wild population of Sumatran rhinos is under 300. This Sumatran rhino calf was born in a zoo. Its life will be different from the life of a Sumatran rhino born in the wild.

Dangers to rhinos

Fewer rhinos are being born, but the main reason rhinos are endangered is that they are being killed by **poachers**. Poachers are hunters who kill wild animals illegally and sell parts of their bodies. Rhinoceros are killed mainly for their horns.

People in some parts of the world still buy rhino horns, even though it is against the law to buy or sell them.

Valuable horns

Rhino horns are used to make dagger handles. A dagger is a symbol of wealth and power in the country of Yemen. People will pay a lot of money for a dagger with a rhino-horn handle!

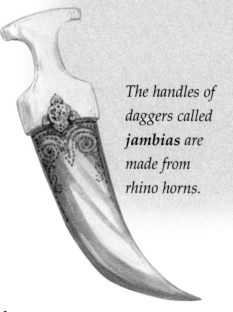

*The handles of daggers called **jambias** are made from rhino horns.*

Asian medicine

Rhino horns are also ground up to make medicine. Some people in Asia believe this medicine helps reduce fevers, but there are many better cures for fevers that do not involve killing rhinos!

Too many people

The human population is increasing everywhere in the world each year. Like animals, people need food. To survive, they are cutting down trees and growing crops where wild plants once grew. They also raise animals such as cattle in the areas they clear. Ruining wilderness areas where wild animals get fresh water and food is called **habitat destruction**. When the plants in areas where rhinoceross live are destroyed, rhinos must compete with people and cattle for food. All rhinos, including the Javan rhino above, are endangered because of habitat destruction.

Living in preserves

Many of the rhinos that live in the wild are in **wildlife preserves** or parks. Preserves and parks are places where several kinds of plants and animals live. They are usually large areas. The rhinos that live in the parks move freely.

The **game wardens**, or people who run the parks, do not feed the animals. They help sick and injured rhinos and try to keep them safe from poachers. In some preserves, armed guards are hired to protect the rhino population.

Operation Rhino

Projects such as Operation Rhino move rhinos from unsafe areas to safer places. In their new homes, rhinos are protected from both habitat destruction and poachers. The white rhinoceros population grew from 20 rhinos to over 12,000 because the rhinos were moved to new parks. The number of Indian rhinos grew from 200 to over 2,000 when these rhinos were moved.

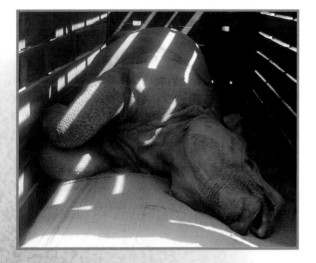

(above) This rhino baby was put to sleep while it was being moved to a safe preserve. It took 15 hours for the trip. (below) The mother rhino was also moved. Twenty people were needed to get her into the truck! Arriving at the park, she backed out of the truck to start a safer life.

Living in zoos

There are not enough wild places for rhinos to live, so many live in zoos. Today's zoos look like the natural habitats in which the animals once lived. The best zoos have teams of scientists who study the animals and keep them safe and comfortable.

You can also learn more about animals by visiting zoos. Many zoos have **species survival plans**. These zoos give rhinos a safe place to live and make babies. With each new calf, the zoos are working to save critically endangered rhinos from becoming extinct.

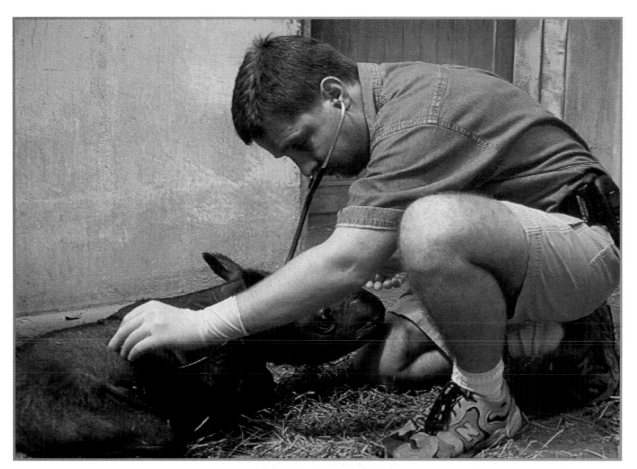

(above) This baby Sumatran rhino was born in a zoo. It is being watched carefully by a veterinarian and other zoo workers to make sure it stays healthy and grows strong.
(right) Sumatran rhinos have patches of long hair, whereas other rhinos are almost hairless.
(opposite page) Newborn Sumatran calves are covered with thick black hair.

29

How you can help

Everyone can help save rhinos. The best way to help is to learn all about them and the places where they live. The more you know, the more information you can share with other people. Then others can also spread the word that rhinos need help!

A great place to learn

If you have a zoo nearby that houses rhinos, ask your teacher if your class can visit. You can learn about how these animals behave and watch them feed and look after their babies.

Fundraising fun

After your visit to the zoo, plan to hold a penny drive, bake sale, or pizza party to raise money to protect your rhino friends in the wild. Perhaps your class can even adopt a rhino!

Extinct is forever!

The best thing you can do, however, is to understand that every animal on Earth is very important to all other creatures, including people. When an animal becomes extinct, it is gone forever! A wonderful way to help animals is by telling others how important they are. These ideas will get you started.

Ways to get started

- With your classmates, start a newspaper about endangered animals. Divide the class into reporting teams and write about the habitats and life cycles of these animals. Investigate which dangers they are facing. Don't forget to include stories about animals that are being saved!

- Take some photographs of rhinos and other endangered animals at a zoo. Use the photos in your newspaper.

- Write poetry about rhinos. Draw pictures to go with your poems and display both on the walls of your school.

Start surfing!

Learn more about rhinos and other endangered animals by checking out **www.nationalgeographic.com/kids**. Look under "Creature Features" to find information on black rhinos.

Click on to **www.rhinos-irf.org** and **www.sosrhino.org** to find out what people around the world are doing to protect rhinos and their habitats.

Try **www.wildlifesearch.com/rhino** to find more great rhino sites.

Glossary

Note: Boldfaced words that are defined in the text may not appear in the glossary. The definitions on page 5 are based on IUCN-The World Conservation Union's Red List of Threatened Species.

charge To attack by rushing forward

habitat destruction The act of damaging the natural place where a plant or animal lives

juvenile Young; not yet an adult

keratin The hard substance that forms beaks, hooves, and nails

lowland Land that is lower or flatter than the land around it

mammal A warm-blooded animal that is born with hair or fur and drinks milk from its mother's body

mate (v) To join together to make babies; (n) A mating partner

predator An animal that hunts other animals for food

species survival plan A program that educates people about endangered animals and brings these animals together to mate in order to increase their populations

submissive Describes a living being that allows another being to control it

territory An area controlled by an animal, person, or group

Index

1 2 3 4 5 6 7 8 9 0 Printed in the U.S.A. 3 2 1 0 9 8 7 6 5 4